THE CHANGING]

Rose Hill

Ann Spokes Symonds

**SERIES
NUMBER
43**

Robert Boyd
PUBLICATIONS

Published by
Robert Boyd Publications
260 Colwell Drive
Witney, Oxfordshire OX8 7LW

First published 2000

Copyright © Ann Spokes Symonds and
Robert Boyd Publications

ISBN: 1 899536 52 3

Printed and bound in Great Britain at
The Alden Press, Oxford

TITLES IN THE *CHANGING FACES* SERIES

	Series no.		Series no.
Banbury: Book One	19	Jericho: Book One	13
The Bartons	34	Jericho: Book Two	39
Bicester: Book One	27	Kennington: Book One	38
Bicester: Book Two	37	Littlemore and Sandford	6
Bladon with Church Hanborough and	18	Marston: Book One	7
Long Hanborough		Marston: Book Two	12
Botley and North Hinksey (Book One)	3	North Oxford: Book One	23
Botley and North Hinksey: Book Two	35	North Oxford: Book Two	30
Chipping Norton: Book One	42	Oxford City Centre: Book One	29
St. Clements and East Oxford: Book One	14	Rose Hill	43
St. Clements and East Oxford: Book Two	17	South Oxford: Book One	24
Cowley (Book One)	1	South Oxford: Book Two	33
Cowley: Book Two	4	Summertown and Cutteslowe	2
Cowley: Book Three	41	West Oxford	22
Cowley Works: Book One	25	Witney: Book One	28
Cumnor and Appleton with Farmoor	10	Wolvercote with Wytham and Godstow	12
and Eaton		Woodstock: Book One	9
St Ebbes and St Thomas: Book One	15	Woodstock: Book Two	21
St Ebbes and St Thomas: Book Two	20	Yarnton with Cassington and Begbroke	32
Eynsham: Book One	16		
Eynsham: Book Two	26		
Faringdon and surrounding villages	40		
Grimsbury	31		
Headington: Book One	5		
Headington: Book Two	8		
Iffley	36		

FORTHCOMING

Abingdon, Bicester: Bk 3, Blackbird Leys, Cowley Works: Bk 2, Easington, Florence Park, Kennington: Bk 2, Kidlington, Littlemore: Bk 2, Oxford City Centre: Bk 2, Wallingford, Witney: Bk 2

. . . and many more!

Do you want to publish a book?

It is not as difficult as you might think. The publisher of this book provides a service to individuals and organisations, large and small.

Advice can be given on all facets of book production.

If you have a project you would like to discuss why not contact:

Robert Boyd
PRINTING & PUBLISHING SERVICES
260 Colwell Drive
Witney
Oxfordshire
OX8 7LW

Contents

Acknowledgements   4

Section 1   Introduction to Rose Hill   5

Section 2   Rose Hill Houses   9

Section 3   Butler House, Margaret House and Alice House   23

Section 4   Rose Hill Methodist Church   26

Section 5   War Memorial and Cemetery   32

Section 6   Community Centre   36

Section 7   Family Centre   51

Section 8   The Allotments   53

Section 9   Singletree Women's Institute   55

Section 10   Dancing, Drama, Sports and Other Activities   57

Section 11   The School   72

Section 12   Shops   76

Section 13   People   81

Cover illustrations

Front: A group of Rose Hill residents taken in the early years of the 20th century.

Back: Bingo in the old hall of the Community Centre taken in about 1957.

Acknowledgements

My thanks go to the many people who kindly provided me with information about Rose Hill. Those who lent me photographs have been acknowledged in the text but I wish to record the names of others who advised me and or gave up their time to talk about their life in this interesting, lively and varied part of Oxford. They include:

Mrs Doreen Alderman, Father Jerome Bertram, CO, FSA, Mr Donald Boyle, Mrs Norman Brown, Councillor and Mrs Bill Buckingham, Mrs A. Burchardt, Miss Frances Cartwright, Mrs Joyce Coveley, Mr and Mrs George Cooper, Ms Jane Creese, Mrs Carol Davis, Mrs Hilda Day, Mrs Ann Ellett, Mrs Margaret Elsey, Mrs Gladys Fagan, Mrs Susan Goldacre, Mr Neil Grant, Mrs Mabel Harris, Mr and Mrs Jeremy Herklots, Mrs Freda Hoare, Mrs H. Kisby, Mrs Betty Ledger, Mrs Gina Marting, Sister Mary of The Work, Mrs Alison Mathias, Mrs Jackie Melson (née Bebbington), Mrs Beryl Mitchell, Mrs E.A. Pearce, Mrs Nora Pearce, Mr David Penwarden, Mr Martin Powell, Mr Keith Price (*Oxford Mail and Times*), Mrs Elsie Rowland, Mrs Janet Simmonds, Dr John Singleton, Mrs Pat Soanes, Mr Peter Stephenson, Mrs Pat Towers, Mr Rick Vellenoweth, Mrs Violet Webb, Mr and Mrs John Wiblin.

My husband, Richard Symonds, has as always been a help and support to me while I was researching and writing this book and he also kindly read the text in draft. I am also much indebted to Dr Desmond Walshaw for his indispensable computer skills and to Dr Milo Shott for his help and expert advice in connection with my photographs.

NOTE ON THE PHOTOGRAPHS

Some of the original photographs were faded or unsharp and did not reproduce well but I have included a few for historical reasons or to illustrate a point. I hope that readers will therefore forgive the quality in order that they can at least gain an impression and be able to appreciate the atmosphere of the place, people or event.

Introduction to Rose Hill

The origins of Rose Hill go deep back in time. People were living in the area as long ago as 100 AD. When the foundations of the Iffley Turn Estate (see below) were being dug by the housing contractors, Messrs Pye Brothers, local archaeologists discovered two potters' fields of the Romano-British period. The area was a convenient place for those who made pots because they could sell them at the edge of the Roman road which ran northwards from Dorchester about two miles from their kiln. The pottery industry also flourished in Roman times in Headington, Littlemore and Sandford.

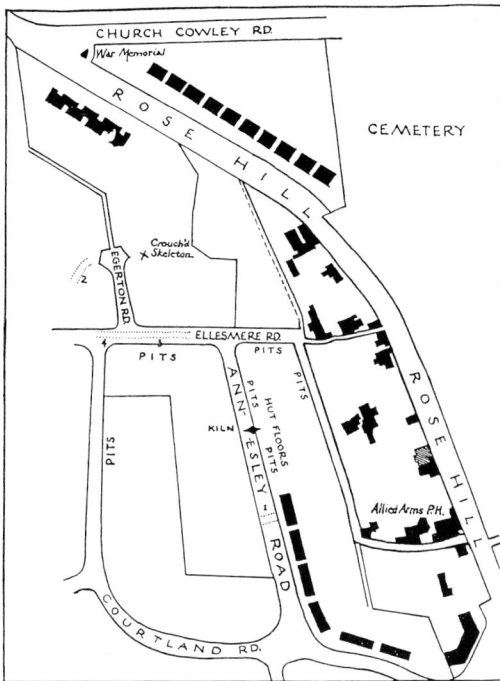

A plan of the excavations undertaken in Rose Hill in the summer of 1935. It accompanies an article by D.B. Harden in *Oxoniensia*, i, 1936, p. 95 under the title 'Two Romano-British Potters-Fields near Oxford' and was published by the Oxfordshire Architectural and Historical Society who own the copyright. It is possible to identify the kiln across Annesley Road and the pits and huts nearby.

It is thought that the kiln was in use during the second century AD although some pottery of the first century was found. Apart from the kiln there was evidence of habitation in the area now covered by Annesley and Ellesmere Roads and this dates from a period between Early Iron Age and Romano-British times. Most of the pottery found was in fragments and came from where the gardens are now on the east side of Annesley Road. Some pits were used for rubbish but others were for cooking purposes. The hut floors east of Annesley Road, near the kiln, were either cobbled with rounded pebbles or made of two or three layers of roughly shaped limestone slabs.

Two coins were found here including one of Constantius II (337–361). A skeleton was found (see plan) by the end of the present Egerton Road and by its position probably dates from pre-Roman times. It is thought that the occupation by the potters lasted until up to the 5th century. The land then remained undeveloped for at least 16 centuries. Some specimens of the pots, including a vase and a dish, are in the Ashmolean Museum.

The turnpike milestone outside No. 37 Rose Hill. It was the 56th stone from London and on it is inscribed: 'London 56, Henley 21, Oxford 2'. The stone, together with a Highway stone further down on the other side of the road (inscribed 'ere — Ifily Hy Way 1635'), are listed of special architectural or historic interest. This was the main road to London via Henley.

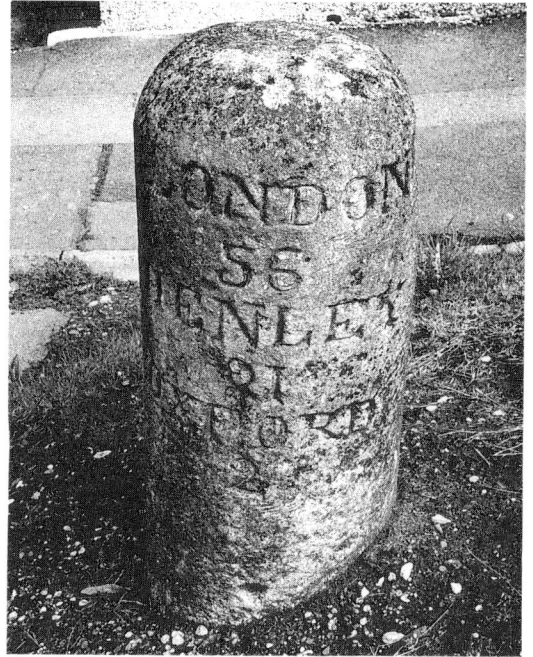

The name of Rose Hill comes from the house in which lived an early 19th century eccentric medical practioner by the name of Ireland. He was the last man in the neighbourhood to wear a pigtail and ruffles at his wrists. He gave the name to his house in about 1800. He died in 1830. He had been anxious that the name should be perpetuated and it was already well established by 1835. The Reverend E. Marshall, in his 1870 account of the area, states that the houses either side of Ireland's were also called Rose Hill when they were built and, on 1st December 1930, the City Council officially gave the road that name.

The Reverend E. Tuckwell, in his *Oxford Reminiscences* of 1900 speaks of Rose Hill Heights as being known to Matthew Arnold. For many years there was a double hedge on the east side. Miss C.V. Butler, in her short history of Rose Hill, published in the Newsletter of the Community Centre *Rose Hill Roundabout* in 1958, wrote: 'In the early 19th century the view from Rose Hill was one of the most beautiful in the world when the spires and towers of Oxford could be observed as one travelled along it between the meadows and cornfields.' This view has not been completely obscured today.

In *Jackson's Oxford Journal* of 27th January 1872, the hope was expressed that 'slight relief will . . . be allowed to a few of Oxford's unemployed' by the cutting of the new road from the bottom of Rose Hill at a turn leading to the Cemetery from the Iffley Road. This meant that the dangerous corner would be eliminated. The City contributed £500 on condition that it went to provide work for unemployed people. By 1921/23 the new road, known as Henley Avenue, had been constructed.

It was the growth of the motor industry at Cowley which was the main reason why the Rose Hill Estate was built. People who had lost their jobs in the Welsh mining industry migrated to Oxford. There was, in any case, a shortage of housing because many of the dwellings in St Ebbe's and St Clement's had been condemned as unfit to live in. Before the coming of the Rose Hill Estate the address of peope living on the hill was 'Rose Hill, Iffley'.

A view of Rose Hill from the air taken on 30th April 1933, courtesy of Miss Betty Mayall. Note the War Memorial on the right edge of the photograph and Iffley Turn at the top.

Tree Lane and Abberbury Road in Iffley can be seen crossing the centre of the picture. Oxford City Council minutes of 1933 recorded the purchase of the land and by 1934 some 150 houses were ready for occupation. It was known as the Iffley Turn Estate. By the beginning of the Second World War the City had built 2000 houses on the estate. In 1947 a second Rose Hill grew up to the south between Iffley and the river with 470 more houses.

An aerial photograph taken in 1947 of the post-war Rose Hill, which was built between the Iffley Turn Estate and Littlemore. The Oval can be seen in the centre of the picture, the river (to the west) at the top and Littlemore bottom left. This was before the Eastern By-Pass was built between Rose Hill and Littlemore.

A writer in the *Oxford Mail* in 1968 bemoaned the fact that the view of the City was not exploited by the Council when they designed the lay-out for this part of Rose Hill. He denigrated the Council for producing a development centred on a windswept space of semi-bald earth which is surrounded by a series of unrelated buildings ... He rudely suggested that Rose Hill was a visual desert which a few cherry trees do little to improve. Now, over 30 years later, the estate is an attractive place with its tall trees and mature gardens. It was one of the fortunate places not to be saddled with a 1960s tower block. Two groups of shops, the school and a thriving Community Centre — one of the best in the City of Oxford — ensure that there is plenty of life in Rose Hill today.

The boundaries of Rose Hill have changed over the years. In 1928, when the City extended its limits, the line went right through the farmers' fields and this is the reason why for many years the housing estate was half in the Iffley ward and half in Littlemore. When the City Council's boundaries were extended once more in 1992 that part of Rose Hill which had been in Littlemore came into the City of Oxford.

Modern transport. The bus terminus at the Oval in 1999.

SECTION TWO

Rose Hill Houses

Singletree

Single Tree, formerly Cingaltree.

When we first took the house the view to Oxford would not have disappointed Matthew Arnold; spires, towers, college roofs ... In the course of a year or so the vision had faded or rather had been killed off by the building of Florence Park Estate. (From *The Pebbled Shore*, the Memoirs of Elizabeth Longford, Weidenfeld and Nicholson, 1986.)

Miss Ethel Loxley (of the Loxleys of the building firm Benfield and Loxley) lived at Cingaltree. However, she eventually found it too large and had another house built next door in 1932 (see below). Cingaltree was then sold to the City Council who leased it out. The house had apparently originally been designed for a chemist who was glad that it looked like a superior college dwelling.

Cingaltree, the tree after which the house was named, the origin of which is not clear. The photograph, courtesy of Mrs G. Fagan, was taken just before the tree was cut down in the 1930s so that the road could be widened. The road widening, completed in 1937, changed the look of Rose Hill.

In 1934 the Pakenhams, as they then were, leased what was still known as Cingaltree from the Council. They changed the name to Singletree. Frank Pakenham represented the Cowley and Iffley Ward on Oxford City Council for the Labour Party between 1937 and 1940. He joined the Army in the Second World War. The Pakenhams did not mind the Florence Park Estate because it was, so Lady Longford explains, filled to the brim with hundreds of Labour voters. Lord Longford himself says that he always considered himself more a Cowley man than an Iffley man.

Antonia, daughter of Elizabeth and Frank Pakenham, and now as well-known an author (Lady Antonia Fraser) as her mother, played as a young child in the large nursery which ran the whole length of the top of the house. Her mother thought that this probably gave rise to Antonia's imaginative mind. She invented two girl companions called Tibby and Tellow.

When the war was imminent, the Pakenhams handed the house over to be used for the evacuees who were beginning to pour out of London. The Council waived the rent and the Pakenhams gave linen, crockery and cutlery. It was chosen as a refuge for a group of blind people from the East End but later more evacuees joined them. By September 1939, when the war started, the Pakenhams left Singletree and went to stay for a time at Water Eaton Manor, north of Oxford.

Sheltered housing in the grounds of Singletree taken in the summer of 1999.

From February 1944, emergency school classes of Juniors and Infants and one Nursery Class were held at Singletree. At their first air raid practice on 1st March 1944, the building was cleared in three minutes. Gas masks were tested about every other month. By 1st May, Annie Wilcox commenced duties as Head. Empire Day was celebrated every year. The Chief Constable visited to give advice on road safety and suggested school signs be erected. The school included for a time some evacuated children and some staff who continued to be employed by London County Council. The piano also belonged to the LCC and when it was returned to them in October 1946, the school had to do without one.

On VE Day there was a 'Cease Fire' holiday for Peace in Europe and the school was closed on 8th and 9th May 1945. On the 10th, a number of children were invited to a 'Victory Hour' by Iffley Women's Institute. In July 1946, the Mayor of Oxford visited and handed out chocolate to 60 lucky recipients. It had been sent by the Optimist International League in Toronto.

Singletree Nursery continued for some years. The Catering and Homecraft department of the Oxford College of Technology, Art and Commerce was also housed at Singletree in the 1950s before it moved to the newly-built College of Further Education in Oxford. Singletree later became an educational resource centre and finally the City Council built sheltered housing on the site, retaining the house itself as part of the scheme. There are 50 self-contained units of accommodation, 21 of which were offered for sale on 99-year leases to people over 60 years of age. The rest was retained for letting by the Council to elderly tenants.

Number 71 Rose Hill was built for Miss Ethel Loxley in 1932/3 and she moved there from what was then Cingaltree next door. In the upper photograph, Pat Fagan, aged about three, who lived opposite at No. 56, is seen as the house was being built. The baker's van belonged to Woodward and Son of Oxford. The Burchardt family lived here from 1949 to 1988. The lower photograph is courtesy of Mrs A. and Mr A. Burchardt.

Number 8 Rose Hill Cottages (later Villiers Lane) was one of the oldest houses in Rose Hill. Unfortunately, it was condemned in 1959 and had to be rebuilt. Bessie (left) and Lily Pulker (see Section 13) are seen at the gate. The washhouse is behind the wall on the left. The photograph, which was probably taken at the time of the First World War, is courtesy of Mrs Doreen Alderman. Both Nos. 8 and 10 were built as labourers' cottages. It was confusing when there were several houses on Rose Hill which had the same number and in 1940 the access road was re-named Villiers Lane, said to be after a former High Steward of Oxford.

Number 10 Villiers Lane taken in the summer of 1999. This was the home of Bill Pulker (see Section 13) from about 1959 when he had moved from No. 8, next door. The pair of cottages had both been condemned at about that time and rebuilt. The Pulkers then sold No. 8 and No. 10 was re-named Rambler Cottage.

Rose Mount, No. 50 Rose Hill, from the north, taken in 1993 (courtesy of Mr and Mrs J. Herklots). From October 1830 to the spring of 1833 this was the home of Mrs Jemima Newman, mother of John Henry Newman (later Cardinal), and her two daughters Harriett and Jemima. They moved here from Brighton to be near John Henry and to help him in his parish and they rented the place from a Mr Eaton. John Henry was Vicar of St Mary the Virgin, the University Church, from 1828 until 1843. The hamlet of Littlemore was part of his parish and Rose Hill was conveniently situated on the way from Oxford to Littlemore. Newman's mother and her daughters created some apartments for him at Rose Mount which consisted of a hall, staircase, study and bedroom and they made a new large window in the study with a view over the garden and a very pleasant outlook towards Oxford. It was at a time when he was to begin some hard reading for a book he had undertaken to write on the history of ecumenical councils. Newman wrote to a friend in July 1831 about his delightful room at Rose Hill from which, sitting in his easy chair, he could see both St Mary's and Iffley churches from opposite windows and thought that 'it is too good for me'.

The south-east corner of No. 50 Rose Hill (formerly Rose Mount) taken in November 1999. There is a plaque high up above the door which gives the date 1791. There was once a conservatory adjoining the window on the left of the front door.

Mrs Newman and her daughters vacated Rose Mount when their lease ended and moved to Rose Bank (now Grove House, Iffley Turn) in the spring of 1833. This portrait of the family by Maria Giberne was probably painted after the move to Rose Bank. Left to right: Francis, Mrs Newman, Harriett, John Henry, Jemima.

John Henry Newman wrote to his mother in April 1833 that he had a natural antipathy to giving names to houses which he thought cockneyish and unnecessary and thought it more respectable for a house to be known by the name of the people who lived there. Because John Henry called the house known as Rose Mount, on the crest of the hill, Rosehill and also called Rose Bank (the name his mothers and sisters preferred) Rosehill, there has been some confusion over the years as to where and when the Newmans lived at these two houses.

Numbers 52 and 54 Rose Hill (see also Section 12).

Villiers Court which replaced Fagan's shop at 56 Rose Hill.

This 19th century house, which was called Rose Villa, with an unusual turret and attractive overlapping oval tiles, is on Rose Hill. The photograph, with Mrs Oram and her grandaughter Samantha Grime, was taken in 1999.

Broomfield, No. 93 Rose Hill. This house had a very happy atmosphere, according to the Hoares who bought it from Magdalen College in 1960 and lived there for 34 years. Dr and Mrs Parkes had lived there before that. This photograph, taken from the garden, is courtesy of Mrs Freda Hoare.

Houses on the main road, Rose Hill, taken in 1999. They were built between 1935 and 1939.

Number 113 Rose Hill taken in about 1997, courtesy of Mrs Susan Goldacre. It was demolished after the death of Miss Mabel Thomas who had lived there for many years.

Orchard Court which was built on the site of Nos. 113–115 Rose Hill. Photograph taken in the autumn of 1999.

Houses in Ellesmere Road, Rose Hill. The road is named after a former High Steward of Oxford as are Egerton and Annesley Roads in the same area, which was originally called the Iffley Turn Estate. The roads were named by Oxford City Council in July 1935. Some of the houses were ready for occupation in 1934 and by the start of the Second World War, 449 houses had been built.

The 'Pre-Fabs', as they were called, were built between 1946 and 1949. Now no longer in existence, they were surprisingly popular with the occupants. Speaking to many former residents who lived in them one realises how much they were enjoyed as homes. They were well-designed and some had big gardens.

The Mitchell Family in front of a pref-fab in about 1954. At the back: Alec Mitchell. Left to right, middle row: Mrs Beryl Mitchell, Mrs Florence Mitchell (Alec's mother) and Mrs Audrey Mitchell (Alec's sister-in-law). A friend is in the chair. Alec was an invalid, having had polio as a child, and he also sufffered from T.B. Beryl was therefore the breadwinner and worked at the Cowley car factory for 25 years.

Above: the pre-fabs in Lambourn Road soon after they were built in the 1940s. The road was named after the well-known Headmaster and writer of history books, E A Greening Lamborn, Hon. MA of Oxford University, but unfortunately the authorities spelled his name wrongly. Ironically, Ikey, as he was affectionately known, often sent back letters if the sender had not spelled his name right.

Left: Beryl Mitchell in the big front garden of her pre-fab in the mid-1950s.

Pat Lindsey on her wedding day
with the pre-fabs behind.

Above and right: two interiors of the Mitchell's
pre-fab taken in 1962. They show the living room
and how light and airy it was. Most had two
bedrooms and there were capacious cupboards.
The houses were made of aluminium. The heating,
which was in the living room, was anthracite, etc.
and was kept on day and night in cold weather.
There was plenty of space and a big hallway. Mrs
Flynn and Mrs Buckell, who both lived in pre-fabs
from about 1946, when their husbands had just
come out of the army, remember them with
nostalgia and as a place where children could
grow up in safety.

One of about 19 Glen Lyon bungalows built in about 1968 in Lambourn Road on the site of the demolished pre-fabs. Although now only a memory, there are many who were sorry to move, even into a new three-bedroomed house. All photographs of the pre-fabs courtesy of Mrs Beryl Mitchell.

Two views of the Rose Hill Estate as it was in 1999. The first shows the north side of Ashhurst Way and the second the corner of Ashhurst Way and Dashwood Road. Ashhurst Way runs between Iffley Road and the Oval, Rose Hill. The name Ashurst, chosen in 1935, commemorates a High Steward of Oxford University who died in 1846. He was also an M.P. Sir Henry Dashwood (1816–1889) was also a High Steward before becoming Lord Lieutenant of Oxfordshire in 1883. Other roads in the area, such as Asquith, Jersey, Spencer and Devereux, are also named after High Stewards.

Orlit houses in Wynbush Avenue. They were originally of concrete slabs with flat tarred roofs. The Council then hip-roofed them with tiles and rough-cast and pebble-dashed the exteriors. Some have been rebuilt. The picture, taken in 1999, shows (right to left) No. 19 (an original

Orlit house), No. 17, an Orlit house which was pulled down and rebuilt, No. 15, an original Orlit, and No. 13 a rebuilt Orlit. There are 105 Orlit houses remaining on the Estate but it has not been possible to discover the origin of the name.

Minnox houses at the foot of Williamson Way in 1999. The shells of the houses were factory-built by Minns, the builders, at Botley. The road, named at the suggestion of the Rose Hill Community Centre, is called after former City Councillor, the Reverend Tony Williamson.

Howard houses in Court Farm Road. The houses were named after the man who invented them. They were factory-made and very well constructed with all iron-girder frames. They were brought to the site on RAF transporters which were called 'Queen Marys' and were normally used for carying aircraft.

The City Council renovated many of the houses in 1989. The original Howard houses had asbestos sheeting covered with rendering. The house on the right is an example of this. Approximately 200 Howard houses remain on the Estate.

The King of Prussia public house

The King of Prussia public house, on the main road, has a complicated and interesting history. King Frederick the Great of Prussia, whose head is on the present-day pub sign, was an extremely popular figure in England in the 18th centruy. His birthday (28th January) was often celebrated in Oxford by the ringing of bells and the lighting of bonfires. Back in the 1750s England and Prussia were close allies in the Seven Years War. It was originally an isolated inn on the lonely Oxford–Henley Road but it is said that the top of the hill is where the post-horses were changed. In 1879 the old inn was replaced by a Victorian building at the cost of £629. It remained there until 1935.

The King of Prussia, Rose Hill, in about 1910. Courtesy of Mr John Fortune. On 16th October 1914, not long after the start of the First World War, the name King of Prussia was replaced by The Allied Arms. An elderly Rose Hill resident, recalling the event some 60 years later, said that a group of soldiers knocked down the old inn sign (which had a portrait of the King of Prussia on it) and it was replaced by that of an English, French and Belgian soldier, representing the Allies. After the Second World War there was a sign showing Churchill, Roosevelt and Stalin but by the 1970s this had been changed yet again to one depicting a golfer, cricketer and rower linking arms.

The 1970s sign. The Co-operative Shop, No. 74 Rose Hill, and Humphris garage now stand on the site of the old Victorian pub.

The present-day King of Prussia, built in 1935 to the south of the old pub, photographed on a winter Sunday morning in 1999.

Butler House, Margaret House and Alice House

Butler House, Ashhurst Way, taken in the summer of 1999. It is the property of Oxford Citizens Housing Association (formerly the Oxford Cottage Improvement Society).

Butler House was named after Miss C.V. Butler (see Section 6) whose book *Social Conditions in Oxford,* published in 1914, alerted people to the bad housing in which the poorer citizens of Oxford lived. Miss Butler served on the Committee of the Society for many years and had also taken part in rent collection.

The history of the Society from its earliest days can be found in *Cottage Improvement to Sheltered Housing* by Robert Mole (1987). The worst housing was found in the low-lying areas of the City which were frequently flooded and were breeding-grounds for cholera, typhoid and T.B. A group of mainly University people therefore came together under the Chairmanship of Dr. (later Sir Henry) Acland, Regius Professor of Medicine. They set up the Cottage Improvement Company Ltd. in June, 1866. Its main purpose was to provide healthy, comfortable dwellings for the labouring classes in the City of Oxford and suburbs thereof.

The directors of the company first concerned themselves with the purchase and repair of old buildings. This was in the days when there was no housing provided by the City Council and in fact the small amount of suitable housing erected before 1918 was all built by private enterprise. It was not until 1934 that slum clearance began in Oxford. In 1958 the City Council allotted the lease of the Rose Hill site, on which Butler House is built, for 75 years. The architect was Mr Thomas Rayson of Oxford. The contract was dogged by problems, including a shortage of bricks, and the fact that the work force kept leaving for better-paid jobs at the Morris Motors and Pressed Steel factories. The house was finally opened on 6th May 1961 with Miss Butler and the Sheriff of Oxford as guests of honour. The cost was £20,689 and rents in the early days were £1 16s a week plus rates.

In 1999 the Oxford Citizens Housing Association managed 1602 units of rented accommodation, 76 bedspaces of shared accommodation and 191 units of shared ownership. The fixed assets of the Society were a total of £30,062,000. I am indebted to the Development and New Business Director of the Association for this further information.

The topping-out ceremony at Margaret and Alice Houses, the Oval, Rose Hill on 2nd August 1968. The group includes, standing by the left-hand table, the Reverend Jonathan Hills, Vicar of Iffley, Miss Joan Scrutton, Secretary of the Cottage Improvement Society, and (on her left) Councillor J.N.L. Baker. Putting tickets in the box is Mr George Cooper. (Copyright *Oxford Mail and Times*.)

Alice Smith, a former resident of Iffley, who had died in 1679, left some land in Littlemore for the benefit of the poor of Iffley parish. The charity had capital for investment and in 1963 the Vicar of Iffley, the Reverend Jonathan Hills, Chairman of the Alice Smith Trustees, approached the Cottage Improvement Society suggesting that they co-operated in building flats for elderly people. The site, at the Oval, was owned by Iffley Church and they sold two thirds of it to the Cottage Improvement Society (later Oxford Citizens Housing). The architects were from the firm of Beecher Stamford Associates of Oxford. The cost of the building was financed by a 100% loan from Bullingdon Rural District Council and the building work was undertaken by Norman Collison (Contractors) Ltd. of Bicester. The total cost was £64,936.

The name Margaret was the first name of Miss Somervell who had earlier given two houses to be sold for the benefit of the Society. The charity's adjoining block was of course called Alice House after the founder.

The offical opening of both blocks was performed by Mrs Michael Flanders on behalf of her husband who was a well-known person with disabilities. Flanders and Swann were members of a very popular double act. The Lord Mayor and Miss Margaret Somervell attended. The scheme was described by the Committee as a remarkable example of co-operation between individuals, an ancient charity and three separate local authorities. There were 15 units at Margaret House and 6 at Alice House and both were managed by the Society.

Two residents of Margaret House who are long-time residents of Rose Hill. On the left is Mrs Bessie Green and on the right Mrs Elsie McCarthy. Photograph taken in October, 1999.

Rose Hill Methodist Church

The Reverend Henry Leake, whose father was listed as one of the Trustees of the Wesley Memorial Church in New Inn Hall Streeet, Oxford, was the founder of Rose Hill Methodist Church in 1835. *The Victoria County History*, (Volume V) does, however, record that Leake had begun his ministry at Rose Hill as early as 1808 when already the Methodists were holding services in the cottage of Mr Gordon, later moving to a tanners yard. Certainly, Henry Leake and his mother came in 1833 to live at Rivermead in Church Way, Iffley.

Finding that the Donnington Trust was unwilling to sell land in Iffley for the new chapel, Leake bought the site of the present church on Rose Hill and paid for the building's construction. The foundation stone was laid in the summer of 1835 at the early hour of 5 a.m. so that people could go to work afterwards. It was known in the early years as Iffley Wesleyan Methodist Church but the forename was changed to Rose Hill in 1843.

Because many in the early congregations could not read, the preacher would recite two lines of a hymn at a time and these would be sung after him. In 1861 the church was transferred by Mr Leake to the United Methodist Free Church Trust. The earliest burials took place in 1842 in the church's own burial ground. In those days practising Methodists could not be buried in Iffley churchyard.

An early view of the Methodist Church, then described as Rose Hill Chapel. In the house on the left was a day school for boys and girls which was founded by Henry Leake. The Master of the school was Benjamin Leonard. This house, and the bank, were demolished when the road was widened. When the Church was built, there were only about 20 buildings on Rose Hill. (Courtesy of Rose Hill Methodist Church.)

The Methodist Church before the graves were moved. (Courtesy of Rose Hill Methodist Church.)

The interior of the Church before renovation. The choir seating visible between the organ and the pulpit has been removed. (Courtesy of Rose Hill Methodist Church.)

The interior of the Church in 1999. (Courtesy of Dr John Singleton.)

The interior of the Church at Eastertide with cross of flowers. On Easter Day members of the congregation come up in turn to place flowers on the cross. (Photograph courtesy of Mrs Freda Hoare.)

The organ

This was presented to the Church in 1893 by the Reverend Reginald John Campbell and a fellow undergraduate at Christ Church, Mr Hignett. Campbell preached his first sermon at Rose Hill. He went on to lead a varied and interesting life, worshipping or ministering in several denominations, and was a prolific writer. He was Minister at the City Temple in London from 1903 until 1915, preaching to large congregations, and was Chancellor and a Canon of Chichester from 1930.

After considerable research, local historian Paul Mayhook believes that there is strong evidence that the organ was originally at St Thomas's Church in Oxford. St Thomas's appointed an organist and purchased an organ around 1840. Experts who have examined the Rose Hill organ believe it was made about that date. Also, the size and casework of this organ fits the site at St Thomas's. That church had ordered a new organ in 1893, making their old one superfluous. Paul Mayhook believes that it is likely that the Reverend R.J. Campbell knew that the organ was available at the time. (Information kindly supplied by Dr. John Singleton.)

In the 1930s, the Church had a Youth Fellowship, an active Christian Endeavour Group, a Boys' Brigade and a Girls' Brigade. The Church also had a long connection with the cause of Temperance and some national pioneers of total abstinence were buried in the churchyard.

The first extension was built in 1940–41 and now forms part of the chancel. This was opened officially on 9th April, 1942 by Miss Gladys Skipper, a member of the church at Rose Hill and Lady Mayoress of Oxford during the Mayoralty of Councillor A.E. Skipper. The second major extension was started in 1957. The church's iron railings were donated to the war effort in the Second World War for which they received compensation of £4 14s 4p.

The choir in 1951. (Photograph courtesy of Mrs Kay Fairman.) Left to right, back row: Mr George Truss, Mr Richard Crossley, –, Mr I. Clamp, Mr K. Clamp, Mr Tim Brown, Mr Horace Foster, Mr Daniel Hart, Mr Fred Bolton. Front row: Mrs Avis Mawer, Mrs Ruth Racey (née Truss), Mrs Truss, Mrs Herring, Mrs Durrant, Mrs Skinner, Mrs Betty Cooper, Miss Gladys Skipper, Mrs Elsie Clamp, Mrs Doris Bolton, Mrs Nellie Foster. Seated in front of the choir on the left is Mrs Wyn Jenkins, the organist, and on the right Mr John Clamp, the choir master.

Some of the choir in 1999 taken by Dr John Singleton. It has revived in recent years; in addition to singing regularly at morning services they have given performances of *Requiem* by Gabriel Faure (1999) and *The Crucifixion* by John Stainer (1998). Left to right, back row: Andrew Blamire. Middle row: Heather Bower, Vicky Tilling, Claire Singleton, Lynne Booker, Jackie Wright. Front row: Laura May Tilling, Rose Booker.

Dr John Singleton, organist and choir master, at the organ of Rose Hill Methodist Church. Taken in 1999.

The new church hall was built behind the church and opened in May, 1958. Among fund-raising activities was that of the Minister, the Reverend Stanley Martin (1951—63), who sat outside Mr Brown's garage opposite Westbury Crescent all day and collected money from members of the public.

The exterior of the church in 1999, taken from the east. Further information can be found in *Rose Hill Methodist Church, 150 Years* by Stephen Roper and Freda Hoare.

A garden party at Broomfield, the home of Mrs Freda Hoare, who kindly lent the photograph, taken in August, 1987. Left to right: Mrs Hulton, Mrs Joan Barnett, Mrs Muriel Fuller, Mrs Freda Hoare, Mrs May Teagle, Mrs Kit Linnell.

Dr G.D. and Mrs Mary Parkes, who were active in the life of Iffley and wrote the history of May Day, lived at Broomfield for many years.

The Church has an active Junior Church and creche and is also the home of the 1st Iffley Guides, 2nd Iffley Brownies and Singletree WI. It also hosts an active weekly fellowship group for retired people known as the Wednesday Fellowship.

The Junior Church (JC) in July 1999, taken by Dr John Singleton. Left to right, back row: George Bower, Heather Bower (JC Helper), Erin Blamire, Coral Blamire (JC Helper), Laura May Tilling, Rosie Wilkinson, Jessica Tilling, Devaine Boyd, Rose Booker, Katherine Blamire, Andrew Blamire (JC Leader), Vicky Tilling (JC Leader). Front row: Joseph Singleton, Louisa Singleton, Amy Cranston, Eleanor Bower, Meghan Blamire, Matthew Booker, Fiona Cranston, Joshua Booker.

The War Memorial and Cemetery

The War Memorial on Rose Hill at the corner of Church Cowley Road, viewed from the west and taken in 1999. Designed by Sir Edwin Lutyens, it is Grade II listed of architectural or historic interest. On the north side the inscription reads: To the Glorious Memory of 5878 of all ranks of the Oxfordshire and Buckinghamshire Light Infantry who fell in the Great War. The inscription on the south side reads: To the Glorious Memory of 1408 of all ranks of the Oxfordshire and Buckinghamshire Light Infantry who gave their lives in the Second World War, 1939–1945. The regiment was represented in every theatre of war in the First World War.

The memorial was unveiled by Major-General Sir John Hanbury Williams, Colonel of the Regiment. It was dedicated by Bishop Shaw on Armistice Day, 14th November, 1923. Because the Bishop took part in the service in St Giles on the same day, this ceremony took place in the afternoon of the 14th. The regimental band accompanied the singing of the hymn 'Oft in Danger'.

Rose Hill Cemetery

In 1883 the Cemetery Committee of the Local Board decided to buy 26 acres of land at Rose Hill from Christ Church in order to make a cemetery. However, because the various parties could not agree on a price it was not until 1889 that the deal went through. By then Oxford had a Corporation which bought ll acres of land from Christ Church at Rose Hill and 13 acres were bought for what is now Wolvercote Cemetery.

Rose Hill Cemetery with its Chapel in the distance.

Close-up of the Chapel. Both photographs taken in 1999. There is a plaque inside recording that the Cemetery was declared open by the Mayor, Aldermen and Citizens of Oxford on March 12 1894. The Reverend J. Magrath, DD, Provost of the Queen's College, officiated at the service of religious dedication. When Dr Magrath died he was buried close by the chapel. The first burial took place on 27th March 1894 and there have been 19,743 burials to date.

The grave of Edward Brooks V.C. in Rose Hill Cemetery. It is understood that he was the only Oxonian resident to receive the V.C. in the First World War. He was the son of Thomas and Selina Brooks and was born on 11th April 1883 at Oakley in Buckinghamshire where his father was a farm labourer.

A copy of the order (No.362) dated 2nd July, 1917, reads

> The Brigadier-General notes with the greatest satisfaction that His Majesty has been pleased to award the Victoria Cross to Company Sergeant Major Brooks, Oxford and Bucks Light Infantry.
>
> By his gallant conduct on the 28th April 1917 Coy Sergt Major Brooks has brought the greatest credit on the 184th Infantry Brigade and has added additional lustre to the splendid historical records of the Oxford and Bucks Light Infantry.

Brooks, once told of his award, immediately wrote a short note to his wife: 'Just a few lines hoping to find you all right and the children keeping well. You will be surprised to hear that I have been awarded the V.C.'

Edward Brooks (who liked to be called Ted) and his wife Elsie (née Danbury) and their eldest child Doris aged about 7. This was taken in 1917.

When Ted returned to Oxford in July 1917, he was given a Reception by the Mayor and Corporation at the GWR station and was driven to Headington accompanied by the Mayor, Brooks' Colonel and Canon Colson, preceded by the Headington Silver Band. The carriage was lent by Mrs Morrell. He was presented with a framed illuminated address for his most conspicuous bravery regardless of personal danger, and also some money which had been collected in the neighbourhood. There were large crowds along the route.

Ted Brooks had a life full of variety. Not wishing to work on a farm he left home at 13 and went to work at Huntley and Palmers biscuit factory in Reading. Unfortunately, when they discovered that he had put up his age a bit they could not continue to employ him officially. However, he was only threatened with dismissal and kept on by the firm, receiving no wages but instead being given a weekly substantial tip. He was there until the start of the Boer War when he was one of the first to volunteer. He was disappointed not be accepted but joined the Brigade of Guards Regiment of Foot at the age of 18½ years for a three-year period. He was able to stand so still when on sentry duty at Buckingham Palace that some American tourists, when trying to rouse him by pushing his buttons in, thought that he must be stuffed. He was a member of the Guard of Honour which welcomed the Kaiser when he came to Britain and later this seemed ironic to him and his family in view of the war which was to come.

After the war was over, Ted left the Army and worked for Lord Nuffield in the days when he was plain William Morris.

The Prince of Wales talking to Ted Brooks during a visit to Morris Motors where Brooks worked from December 1919 until his death in 1944.

In the Second World War Brooks wished to be a dispatch rider, this time putting his age back instead of forwards, but without success.

Ted Brooks died at his home in Morrell Avenue on 26th June, 1944 aged 61 years. Brooks Taylor Court in Albion Place, St Ebbe's was named after him and for a member of the Womens Army Corps. It was built by the Royal British Legion Housing Association.

All information and photographs courtesy of Ted Brooks' daughter, Mrs Nora Pearce.

The Community Centre

The first Centre at Rose Hill was founded on 5th July 1937, only two years after the earliest tenants came to live in the new municipal housing near Iffley village. After the Housing Act of 1936 local authorities were allowed to set aside land on their new estates for the needs of the community, including recreation. The Oxford Council of Social Service, which was a voluntary body, was allocated a plot of land off Ashurst Way, near the Spencer Crescent turn. A capacious wooden building was put up at a cost of £400 to house the centre, which was expected to be temporary. It was the first of its kind in the City. Miss C.V. Butler (see below) did much to encourage its foundation.

The hall of the centre was 60 feet long and there were two adjoining rooms. £250 was raised by voluntary subscriptions and donations and the deficit was met by Alderman L.H. Alden in his capacity as Mayor of Oxford and President of the Council of Social Service. At the 1937 opening ceremony the Mayor knocked at the door which was opened by two little girls, Betty and Hilda Roberts, who asked him to enter.

Members of the first Committee were keen to start events at once. Mrs L.M. Parker, one of the first members, later wrote about the club for girls between the ages of 5 and 10 which she started in 1937 and which met on Wednesday nights. The club had no money but the girls paid a penny and made small garments etc. which, with the sale of lemonade, made sure it did not run into debt.

Dances were held at the Centre on Saturday nights from the beginning with people paying 6d a head. It did not quite cover the cost of the band but people made up the deficit out of their own pockets. 'The word, at the time' Mrs Parker wrote, 'was Onward.' Other activities to begin almost at once were a weekly welfare centre for babies and also Scouts and Wolf Cubs which were started by Miss M. Huxley in 1937/38.

The Local Education Authority (Oxford City Council) sanctioned the appointment of a part-time Warden for the Centre in 1940 but it was not until two years later that they paid the full cost of the part-time salary. At about this time the City Council took over the running of the Centre from the OCVS. Miss D. M. Jackson from Barnett House, the Oxford Centre for Training in Social Work, was the first Warden and held office between 1940 and 1947. In fact, she worked much more than part-time. It was she who said in 1943 that the Centre was the only integrating influence upon a heterogeneous group of people who need to build up a tradition of community and neighbourliness and culture that accompany it.

By 1943 there was a twice-weekly Nursery Centre for toddlers, Infant Welfare, Junior and Senior boys and girls clubs and a mixed club for girls over 13 and boys over 14. There were Scouts and Wolf Cubs, Girls Service Cadets, a Women's Co-op Guild, Women's Club and Keep Fit Classes, an Adults Discussion Group (led by the University Extra-Mural Department), Saturday Socials and Dances, Sunday School, Church services, meetings of elderly people, the Allotment Association and a weekly Citizens Advice Bureau. A good and cheerful municipal restaurant served midday meals and there was an air raid wardens post in the grounds of the Centre. From its early days the Community Association had a democratic constitution with a Management Council.

In 1949, Mr Alec Briggs was appointed as a full-time Warden.

The first Community Centre was burnt down on 15th March 1955. Starting at 3 a.m., the cause of the fire was never found. Mr Briggs said that it was an awful shock and that he did not know what people would do. As he explained: Practically everything takes place here from the welfare of old people to whist drives, drama groups, youth movements and Sunday schools. By 10 a.m. the next day women with mops and buckets came to clear up. Undergraduates of St Anne's and Oriel colleges, who had had links with the Centre for some years, helped with money and personal help connected with the Youth Club. Committee meetings were held in the home of Mr Bill Buckingham in Court Farm Road.

The needs of Rose Hill for a new centre, foreseen in the Oxford Development Plan, were soon voiced. It was recognised that Rose Hill had been the pioneer community centre in Oxfordshire. These needs were represented strongly to the City Council by Councillor Percy Bromley and others, and the Council agreed to earmark £13,000 for a new centre to be built on the Oval which was just outside the City boundary.

Above, the Community Centre (north side) and, below, with the bus terminus, the south side, showing part of the extension. The first phase, designed by Oxford City Council Architects department, was opened in September 1956 by Alderman Allaway (Mayor 1956/7). The photographs were taken in 1999.

Mr K. Whiteside was appointed Warden in 1956 with Miss A. Daniel as Assistant Warden.

Miss C. Violet Butler (1884–1982), a tutor at St. Anne's College, Oxford, seen here presenting a cut-glass bowl to Mrs. Bullock for long service. Miss Butler was an indefatigable worker behind the scenes. She attended Committee meetings from the time the Community Association was formed in 1937. Those parts of the Centre's activities nearest to her heart were the Youth Club for girls and the Silver Threads (for older people), which is still running under that name. She bought a Nissen-type hut which she presented to the Girls' Club so that the girls could have their own place. When in 1957 people at the Centre heard that she had written a book (in 1912) entitled *Social Conditions in Oxford*, the Centre's magazine reported it as a case of hidden talent. She was, in fact, as the article on her in the *Dictionary of National Biography* by Brian Harrison tells us, the first woman at Oxford University to get a distinction in the diploma in economics and political science. She could also speak four languages. She was a pioneer of English Social Work training which few Rose Hill people knew about. On the right in the picture is Councillor H.G.L. Gordon-Roberts, Mayor of Oxford in 1958, and on the left is Mr Norman Brown, for many years Chairman of the Community Association, an active participant in Rose Hill affairs and the talented Editor of its Newsletter *The Rose Hill Roundabout*.

Photographs taken at the Community Centre are courtesy of Mrs Babs Brown.

A group taken at a Community Centre party at the same time as the previous photograph with the Mayor and his lady seated and Miss Butler, Mrs Bullock and Mr Brown again in the picture. Standing in the back row 4th from left is Mr F.S. Green, Community Services Organiser, Oxford City Council Education Department, and 6th from left Mr Bill Buckingham.

Dancing in the old Community Centre hut in the late 1940s.

A party in the old hut in 1951.

Right: Community Centre girls on 21st March 1951. Miss Betty White (left) was chosen as Miss Rose Hill and Miss Sylvia Lovelock as Miss Cowley.

Below: enjoying a game of cribbage in the Centre. Left to right: Andy Brown, Cyril Townsend, Tony McCullough, Norman Brown, Ron James.

Bingo in the old hall, now the Ballroom, in about 1957. Mrs Nellie Baker is holding up the winning number. (Copyright Rose Hill Community Centre.) In the picture on the left, with hand near chin, is Mr Springer and, at bottom right, Mr East, with hand to face, Mrs East, in white dress, and, on her left, Mrs Woodward.

Bingo in more recent times (1999) at the Community Centre where it is still played regularly. Here is Mr George Cooper in charge. Ask anyone who has done the most for the community over the years and the first name on many people's lips will be that of George Cooper. He was Warden from 1964. In 1974 he became Senior Education Worker (Oxfordshire County Council) at the Adult Education Centre at Peers School, but advising the Centre was still part of his job. After the retirement of Mr Cooper in 1983 Mr Alan Noble, who was also at the Peers Centre, continued to advise until 1998. George still plays an active part in Centre affairs and is one of those who has done much to cement good relations between Rose Hill and Iffley.

Playing Bingo are, left to right, Mrs V. Mold, Mrs. P. Hayden, Mrs M. Randles, Mrs. B. M. McCartney, Mrs R. Briggs, Mrs E. Wyatt. In front: Mrs I. Pladys.

Left to right: Mrs R. O Malley, Mrs M. Sykes, Mrs G. Miles, Mrs V. Hirons, Mrs. G. Stebbings.

Mrs M. Flynn, Mrs. E Timmins, Mrs K. Tallon, Mrs G. Little.

These photographs of Bingo at the Rose Hill Community Centre were taken in 1999.

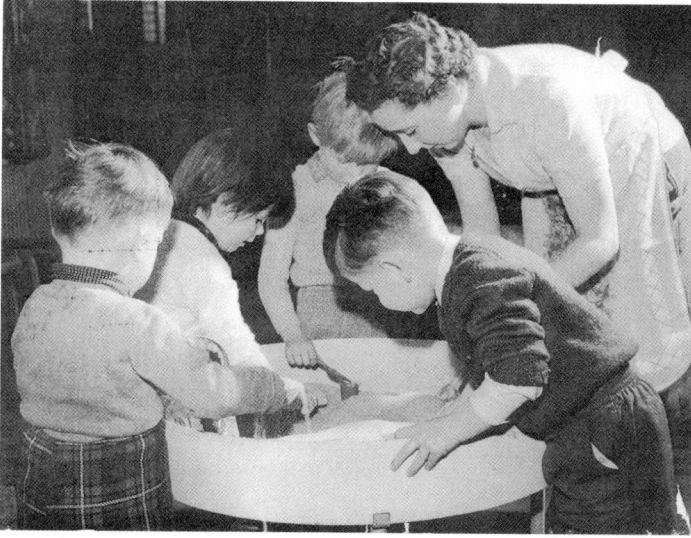

The Toddler Group in 1963 with Mrs Buchanan, the founder. The Group was re-started in the late 1960s by Mrs Freda Cooper.

Playing in the sand at the Toddler group, 1963.

A group of children at the Playgroup (formerly the Toddler Group) in 1999. It is open Mondays to Fridays from 9.30 a.m. to 11.45 a.m. Left to right: back row: Aoub Benkaem, George Brook, Alexander Day, Laura Duggan, Steven Jackson, Luke Jackson, Amy Newport, Claddagh Gaughan. Front row: Zoe Thompson, Oliver Davis, Luke Henbury, Audrey Pautrat, Craig Honey, Liam Wyatt, Sophie Perkins.

The staff at the Playgroup. Left to right: Lynn Davis (parent helper), Iris Bunyan, Maxine Holmes (parent helper), Gina Marting (Supervisor), Janet Spiers, Lorna Skelcher.

Activities at the Playgroup. From left: Aoub Benkaem, Steven Jackson on Maxine Holmes' lap, Laura Duggan, Kaine Parsons with Janet Spiers. Foreground: Amy Newport, Lorna Skelcher.

Left to right: Laura Duggan, Kaine Parsons, Janet Spiers.

Left to right, back: Zoe Thompson, Craig Honey (on bicycle) Alexander Day. Front: Claddagh Gaughan, Iris Bunyan.

Claddagh Gaughan painting. All the Playgroup photographs were taken in 1999.

Members of the Youth Club in the late 1950s.

A children's party in the Centre in about 1967. Mrs Townsend is handing out the food.

The Annual Dinner of the Rose Hill Community Association on 28th September 1960. Left to right, at top table: Mrs. R.O. Baker, Mr K.D. Baker, Mrs T. McCulloch, Mr McCulloch, Mrs Bromley (Lady Mayoress), Alderman Percy Bromley (Lord Mayor), Mr Norman Brown (standing), Chairman, Mrs Norman Brown, Mr K. Whiteside (retiring Warden), Mrs Whiteside, Mr F.H. Cottell. Mr Whiteside had recently been appointed to a new post at Poole after 4½ years at Rose Hill. Even at this time the Centre was described as one of the biggest and most flourishing in Oxford. A presentation was made to Mr Whiteside at the dinner.

A jolly get-together; a social evening at the Centre in the early 60s.

A social occasion in the late 1960s. In the centre are Mr and Mrs Adams and on the right is Mrs Dot Fowler.

Helpers at a Community Centre Bazaar in the later 1960s. Left to right: Mrs Doreen Shepherd, Mrs Congdon, Mrs Babs Brown.

Another evening social occasion in the early 1970s. Second from left: Mrs Barber, fourth from left Mrs Parsons and far right Mr George.

**ROSE HILL COMMUNITY
ASSOCIATION**

Adult Social Club

Meetings every Thursday
8 p.m. — 11 p.m.

Fully Licensed

PROGRAMME

FOR

JANUARY to APRIL 1969

THE OVAL
ROSE HILL
OXFORD   Phone. Oxford 77542

JANUARY

2nd	Normal Club Night
9th	Adult Social Club Annual General Meeting
8 p.m.
16th	Normal Club Night
23rd	Twenty Questions—Animal, Vegetable or
Mineral—Question Master: G. B. Cooper, Warden
30th	Pantomine Outing–New Theatre, Oxford
"Babes in the Wood"
Coach will leave the Centre at 7 p.m.

FEBRUARY

6th	Debating Group 7.30 p.m.
Subject to be announced later
Chairman: The Rev. Paul King
13th	The Motor Club present a
GRAND VALENTINE DANCE 8–11.45 p.m.
Dancing to the "Gaytours"
Fancy Dress Optional– Dressing Rooms available
for changing.
Prize for Best Dressed Lady and Gentleman
Judging by Local Personality
Bar extension to 11.15 p.m.   Admission 8/
including Refreshments, Tickets limited
20th	Jackie Bebbington Pantomine at 7 p.m.
"Dick Whittington"

Adults { reserved   3/6   Chld'n { reserved   2/6
{ unreserved 3/-   { unreserved 2/-

27th	Helper's Party

MARCH

6th	Normal Club Night
13th	Your Garden 7.30 p.m.
Speaker — Slides — Questions
20th	Social Evening with another Club
Details to be announced later
27th	Community Association Annual General
Meeting, 8 p.m.
Social afterwards – Dancing to Music of Ray & Bern
Refreshments at moderate charges

APRIL

3rd	Easter Gala 8–11.45 p.m.
Dancing to the Music of the Oxford Show Band
Bar extension to 11.15 p.m.
Non-Members 12/6 } including buffet
Members 10/6 }
Book early to avoid disappointment
10th	Members' Bingo 7.30 p.m.
17th	Entertaining Cutteslowe Community Assoc.
24th	Dinner Out at New Inn, Shillingford
Full details to be arranged later. Approx. 22/6d.

Other than where a Bar extension has been
granted—Local Licensing Laws will be observed.

Programme of the Adult Social Club for January—April 1969.

Today the Centre is still one of the most active and well-run in Oxford. In 1994 the Association paid off a loan of £130,000 from the brewery which had been borrowed in order to build an extension to the buildings. The Playgroup and the Silver Threads were two of the groups meeting in this new wing. The Dawson Trust (St Clement's) and the Doris Field Trust (Headington and Marston) have helped with grants to the Centre in recent years. The whole Centre is a hive of activity and it still plays an extremely important part in the life of Rose Hill. It has certainly fulfilled the wishes of the first Warden made in 1943 and has built up a tradition of community and neighbourliness.

The Rose Hill Garden and Social Club

The Rose Hill Garden and Social Club Show has been going for 35 years. It used to be run by the Allotments Association about 30 years ago.

Guessing the weight of the marrow at the September 1999 Show held at the Community Centre. Left, Mrs Babs Brown and, right, her daughter Carol Davis. Mrs Joan Pugh is seated in the foreground and Mrs Goodwin is at the hatch.

Left, Mrs Beryl Hastings (Chairman) and Mrs B. Mitchell (Secretary and Vice-Chairman) of the Garden and Social Club. They are checking the Show entries which have won prizes.

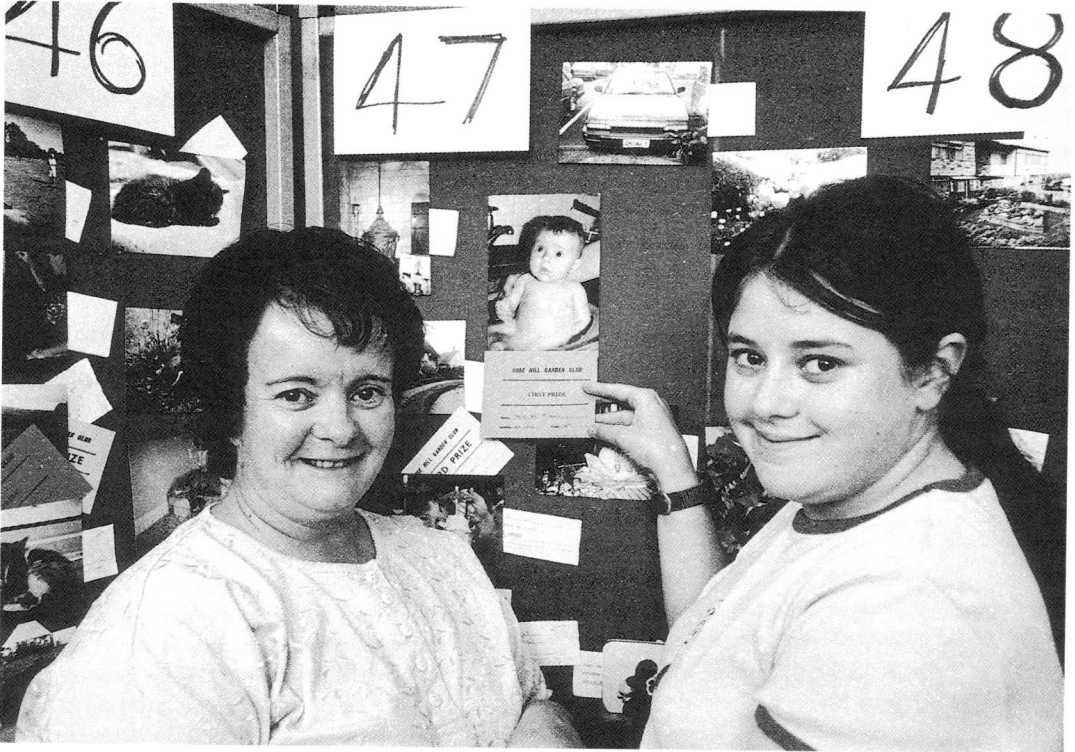

Mrs Maureen Evans, left, and her daughter Gemma at the 1999 Show. They won a first prize for the photograph of Gemma taken as a baby.

Councillor Bill Buckingham with the cups and trophies which he later presented to the prizewinners at the Rose Hill Garden and Social Club Show in September 1999.

Family Centre

The idea for a Family Centre was put forward by the Head Teacher of Rose Hill First School and it was opened in 1989.

The Centre aims to be a friendly and informal place where all the family are welcome and where people can meet their friends or meet new ones. Not only are courses available in such subjects as English and Maths, but there are two parenting programmes and more recently a Credit Union has been set up. Advice on welfare and legal rights is also available. The Centre is funded by Oxfordshire County Council and grant aided by Oxford City Council.

Recently, the Centre was chosen by the Government to be part of a new initiative called Sure Start which will incorporate a new building and with the specific aim to work with 0–3 year olds and their families. Older groups will still continue, including the After School Club and other local initiatives. Information about the Centre kindly supplied by its Head, Jane Creese.

Parents and children outside the Family Centre on 19th February 1993. Left to right: Michelle Allen with Naomi, Sue with Michael, Susan Hannon with two foster children, Samantha Webb with Ruby and Sophie, ?, Christine Twist with Amy, Debbie Yeates with Thomas. (Copyright *Oxford Mail and Times*.)

A group at the Family Centre in the summer of 1999. Left to right: Abbey Twist, Ann Ellett, Yvonne Orman, Yarmohamed Majia with Yusef Majia, Carrie-Ann Watton with Aaliyah Townsend, Karen Watton, Jan Mcleod.

The Allotments

Rose Hill Allotments in Lenthall Road are situated on part of the former Glebe land which Oxford City Council bought from the Anglican Diocese just after the Second World War. They form a natural boundary between Iffley Village and Rose Hill and are cultivated by both communities, together with a growing number of post-graduate students and young people with families. The site has fine views of the spires and towers of Oxford as well as of the hills to the west. Made up of 88 plots, there is piped water to drums near each of them. There is also a plumbed toilet and a site shop. Other amenities include a communal lawn and a large cedar shed situated in the centre of the 6.71 acre site. There is also a sand-pit and a supply of childrens toys.

In 1999, the Allotments Committee organised two barbecues which were attended by 60 allottees and their families. It is intended that these will continue to be an annual social event to bring together plot-holders. Until the 1980s, the main social event was a winter dance in the Rose Hill Community Centre which was usually attended by the Lord Mayor. However, ballroom dancing has now declined in popularity.

Two photographs of a barbecue at the Allotments in the summer of 1999. From left to right: Lydia Penwarden, Wendy Rees and (behind) the Reverend W. Brooker, Methodist Minister, talking to Lorraine, a post-graduate student. Michael Fernandez (at the table) talking to Helen Matten (back to camera).

Left to right at front: Lydia Penwarden, Wendy Rees, Michael Fernandez (in the baseball cap), Helen Matten and others. (Both photographs by David Penwarden.)

In recent years, women in particular have introduced changes to the traditional vegetable plot. Gooseberry and currant bushes have been introduced together with varieties of dwarf fruit trees. Garden seats encourage family picnics and the intricate patterns of stone paths give an architectural dimension to the plots which are traditionally 10 poles in size. Broad grass paths laid on hardcore give good access and are well maintained by Michael Fernandez, the Field Secretary, who has attended daily since retiring from the Oxford University Press. He now has a sit-on mower, a strimmer and a supply of woven plastic sheeting which is used to suppress weeds on uncultivated plots. Michael came to Oxford via Goa and Uganda and has been delighted to discover that many staples of Indian and African cuisine grow just as well in Rose Hill. He offers them freely to members and they form the basis of his famous chutneys and samosas. Garlic, coriander, turmeric, fenugreek and Jamaican spinach thrive among the more traditional herbs and vegetables.

A group of Allotment holders on a November afternoon in 1999. Left to right: Mr and Mrs Gordon Hall, Michael Fernandez, David Penwarden and Ken Rees.

At their 1999 AGM, members decided to offer quarter-size plots for the first time and discussed the possibility of establishing a community orchard. Associate members already use the site shop and an artist simply paints the views. As David Penwarden, Trustee and President of the Lenthall Road Allotments, says: It is a far cry from digging for victory or eeking out a paltry pension.

I am much indebted to David Penwarden for the information about the Allotments.

SECTION NINE

Singletree Women's Institute

This thriving Institute was formed in July, 1973 when Mrs Sussana Fuller was elected as the first President. Meetings are held in the hall of the Rose Hill Methodist Church.

Mrs Susanna Fuller (President 1973–1976). Her lace-making classes, which were held all over the County, were often over-subscribed. (Photograph by Tim Nuttall)

Singletree W.I. members in fancy dress on St George's Day 1987. The photograph was taken outside Rose Hill Methodist Church. Left to right, back row: Aline Hayden, Caroline Jordan, Gwen Shaw, Ann Robinson (holding paper), Gwyneth Jenkins (wearing a mortar board). Front row: Bess Wright, Olive Molden, Phyllis Long, Nell Williams, Alice Richardson, Joyce Westlake, Eileen Brooker, Eve McCarthy.

The Institute's 18th Birthday Party in July, 1991. The cake is being cut by, left to right: Mrs Joyce Westlake (former President) Mrs Helen Kisby (President), Mrs Eileen Smith (former President).

Two founder members of Singletree W.I. taken in 1998 at the 25th Anniversary Party. Mrs Ivy Godfrey (left) and Mrs Dot Phillips.

Dancing, Drama, Sports and Other Activities

A group of Jackie Bebbington's School of Dancing (JBSD) in the old hut of the Community Centre in the early 1950s. Jackie has been teaching dancing at Rose Hill for nearly 50 years. Before the Centre was built at Rose Hill, the classes were, for a while, held at Singletree. Over the years the children have raised thousands of pounds for local charities. An average of £800 has been collected for Rose Hill School each year for the last 14 years. In the front row of the photograph are: second from left Mavis Dalloway, fourth from left Jackie Roper, sixth from left Carol Collins, seventh Christine Beecham. On the far right is Linda Comben. In the third row are: third from left Margaret Whiteman, fourth Julie Maskell, eighth Veronica Jenkins, tenth Diane Swain.

JBSD girl tap-dancers dressed as soldiers. Left to right: Jennifer Shirley, Georgina –, Margaret Whiteman, Diane Swain, Sandra –.

Presentation to Jackie Bebbington after a performance of Snow White and the Seven Dwarfs in the 1950s. Curtsying, left, is Wendy Gibbons who presented the bouquet. Jackie produced a Pantomime each year in the late winter.

Two scenes from Cinderella produced by Jackie Bebbington in the 1960s.

JBSD girls in the 1960s. Tap-dancing is, with Judo, one of the longest-running activities at the Centre.

Girls of JBSD in a tableau at the Community Centre in the 1960s. (All the above photographs courtesy of Jackie Bebbington.)

Jackie Bebbington's girls at the Community Centre in 1999, again posing in tableau form. Left to right, back row: Cheryl Moore, Rebecca Thorne, Emma Brown, Steffani Hall, Hannah Matten. Front: Kayleigh O'Callahan, Katie Matten.

Boys' football team, Rose Hill, 1958/59.

Girls' football team, Rose Hill Community Centre, in the 1960s. Fifth from the left is Judith Allison.

A game of Whist in the old hut in the late 1950s. This was a popular game for many years.

The three photographs above by courtesy of Mrs Babs Brown.

Youth Club Weightlifting Section in the late 1960s or early 1970s.

Scottish dancing at a Community Centre Fête in the early 1960s which was held in the grounds of the school.

Girls doing a knees-up in the old hut in the 1950s.

Fêtes were held regularly. In 1963, Alderman Alec Parker, the Lord Mayor of Oxford, is here considering on which square he is going to sign his name. On the right is Ann Congdon, now Mrs Simpson.

The girls' race at a Fête in the 1960s.

The boys' race. Vic Mobley (on the left) became a well-known footballer.

A running race at the Fête of 1963 in the grounds of Rose Hill School.

1963, Wheel of Fortune. Running the wheel, and talking to the Lord Mayor, is Mrs Boddington, member of the Community Centre, and in the background (behind man with pipe) is Mr Reg Baker, Chairman, Community Association.

Roll-a-Penny at the 1963 Fête with the Lord Mayor looking on.

Throwing the dice at a Fête in the 1960s.

Watching the running races at Rose Hill in the 1960s.

The Lady Mayoress judges a fancy dress competition at the Centre Fête in 1963.

Girls and boys playing tug o' war.

Skittles. Tommy McCullough is sending down the heavy wooden ball. Left to right, back: Alec Goodwin, Brian Simpson, ? McHenry, Mr Cook, Mr J. Bachmann (J.B.), Bob Arnott, Mrs Doreen Shepherd, Mrs Babs Brown. Front: Dot Goodwin, Dora McCullough, Norman Brown, Nellie Baker, Ida Blomfield, Vera Jackson, Muriel Brown, Reg Baker. Date not known. (Photograph copyright *Oxford Mail and Times*)

Skittles in 1957/58. Left to right, back row: Norman Brown, Nellie Baker, Reg Baker, Cyril Cooper, Andy Brown, Norman Brown, Jr., Jack Congdon. Bowling is Ken Boddington. Behind him is (left to right) Dot Fowler, −, Mrs Muriel Brown, Mrs Shepherd, Mrs Babs Brown, with Mr McCullough behind her, Jean Brown, Mrs Goodwin, Mrs Cooper, Mrs Boddington. Kneeling in front is Mr Goodwin.

A Keep Fit Class, date not known. Front to back, left-hand row: −, −, −, −, Jennifer Lanefor, Patsy White, Chris Treadwell. Middle row: Joan Wigmore (Instructor), −, −, −, Joan Wyatt. Right-hand row: Nesta Morris, −, Jean Jenkins, Pat Soanes, Jane ?, Rosemary French.

Judo is one of the longest-running activities. This was taken in the Community Centre in the 1960s. It is still going strong today.

Judo at the Community Centre in 1999. (Photographs by the author. Courtesy of Mr Neil Grant.) Left to right: Andrew Wren, Neil Grant, Damion Cox, Nick Thorne, Paul Oakley.

Left to right: Paul Oakley (on the floor), Nick Thorne (throwing) Andrew Wren, Damion Cox, Neil Grant.

Girls doing needlework in the late 1960s. Geraldine Avery is on the far left.

Dressmaking in the late 1960s. Left to right: —, Nellie Baker, Mrs Phillips, making her long dress.

Showing off the dresses which they had made. Second left is Janet Jackson (now Mrs Griffiths); fifth left is Linda Combun.

Dressmakers showing their handiwork. Reading out the results is Mrs King, Instructress. Note that Mrs Phillips is wearing the long dress she was shown making on the previous page.

Photographs are courtesy of Rose Hill Community Centre unless otherwise stated.

The School

Part of Rose Hill First School, taken in 1999.

The school was built in a period of post-war optimism on a large piece of land at the Oval in the centre of the Rose Hill estate.

Although the primary school had already come there in January 1951 (by May 1952 the numbers had reached 300) the official opening did not take place until 10th July, 1952. About 200 parents and 80 official guests assembled in the main hall to hear Mr John Christie, Principal of Jesus College, Oxford, give his speech opening the school. The audience must have been slightly surprised that this former Headmaster of two Public Schools assured them that nowhere in such schools as Winchester and Westminster would such fine classrooms be found as those at Rose Hill. Annie Wilcox, Head of the Infants, who had come on there from Singletree, summed up the situation by saying: 'Believe me, this vast building is a fearful place for a small child who has spent all his days in the comfort of a small house.'

Certainly the school in its early days was something of a show piece. The visitors book records delegations coming from all over the world to see it, including Denmark, Switzerland, Sweden, Germany, Australia and British Guiana.

A school group taken in the early years of the school, probably in 1952 or 1953. Mr Kitchen is the teacher (centre back) and the boy in front of him is John Phipps. Front row: —, —, Doreen Leach, Wendy Wyatt, —, Janet Woodfield, Linda Whiteman, —, —.

John Phipps remembers that in the early years of the school, children were given little canvas bags to take home at the end of one of the terms. In the bag were gifts such as a small ball or a little book. These were much appreciated by the children.

At first the school was divided into infants and juniors. Mr Frederick Henry Catttell was Head of the latter. By September 1955, there were 355 children on the roll. Many of them had transferred from Singletree (see Section 2) and they came with their teachers to this new school. In the 1950s there was no playing field, just a concrete playground. The infants from Singletree moved to Rose Hill in January 1952.

By 1975, when the Middle School system was phased in, Rose Hill became a First School with transfer at nine years of age to middle schools. The two schools, junior and infant, had, by 1973, already merged to become an 'all-through' Primary school under Mrs C.P. Norman who had earlier been Head of the infants.

Some examples of school life can be found in the log books. In September 1952, for instance, a school uniform was introduced in maroon and turquoise (later changed to navy) with caps for boys and berets for girls and badges and ties for both. By June 1954, it was recorded that staff were worried because children were coming to school tired after staying up late to watch television. Parents were asked to co-operate and supervise their children's viewing.

Many concerts were held through the years and the school choir seems to have been especially strong. Regular medical inspections were undertaken by Dr John Warin, Medical Officer of Health. He and his family happened to live not far away in Iffley. By 1st January 1967, the school had its own branch library.

In 1959, a teacher was severely reprimanded for using a slipper on the buttocks of two children as a punishment. Although corporal punishment was still permitted, it could only be given by the Head (or a teacher appointed by the Head) and it had to be entered in the punishment book. Recently, a visitor came to the school who said he was once a pupil there and the Head suggested that he look up his name in the behaviour book. However, the visitor assured him that his name would not be found in it. Nevertheless, his name *was* found with the entry

'P.C. was throwing ink pellets at the wall and received one stroke.'

The culprit is now a University lecturer and has a Ph.D.

Although the buildings may have been in advance of their time, the log book records continual problems, especially throughout the 1950s and 1960s, with the heating system. The flat roof caused the most problems.

Pupils at the school with some musical instruments in February 1999. Left to right, back row: Zara Moore, Nicola Edwards, Kurt Kauble, Scott Butler, Chase Mullins, Lewis Adams. Middle row: Heather Davis, Christopher Bateman, Nathan Pill, Daniel Saxton, Christopher Berger, Barry Williams. Front row: James Gallagher, David Collier.

There were 333 children on the school roll in 1999, mostly between the ages of 5 and 9, but this number also included the Nursery where they were mainly 4-year olds.

The School Language Resource Base is at Rose Hill. It is for those with speech and language difficulties and, in 1999, consisted of about 26 children. They have daily speech therapy but for some activities they are integrated with the rest of the school.

The school also has a scheme called Parent Watch in which volunteers carry out casual surveillance of the buildings. Parents and staff work together to try to prevent vandalism which has been reduced as a result by 75%.

The Hamilton Trust, founded by Mr Michael O'Regan, supports the school by providing computers, books and additional training. It has become an integral part of the school. Clergy from the Church (St Mary's, Iffley) come to the school once a month for a service. About 30 volunteers from Iffley help and support the school in all sorts of ways and are kind and benevolent friends. These volunteers have been mentioned in a new booklet published by the Quality Performance Improvement Division of the Department of Education and Employment, and Rose Hill is the first school to be featured in this guide to good practice. The mathematics work at the school has also been highlighted in two other national publications. The classroom helpers typically spend from two to four hours a week working with the children. The school is now also part of Oxfordshire's first Education Action Zone.

The Head Teacher at Rose Hill School, Mr Peter Stephenson, says that it is 'a challenging community with a great deal of work still needing to be done to lift the spirits of so many people on this detached estate.' Nevertheless, he is optimistic and says 'Academic attainment has improved over the last few years and the school is on the move.'

Shops

The Cracknell family with some of their friends at the opening of their shop on Rose Hill by Emily Cracknell (née Cherry) in 1914. This was in the year in which they came to Oxford. She died in 1918. Left to right, back row: Mr Surman, Coach driver, —, —. Front: —, a German evacuee, Gladys Cracknell (9 years old), Harry Cracknell, two Thompson brothers, George Henwood, Emily Cracknell.

Mrs Cracknell also worked at St Hilda's College and Gladys recalls that at that time the family lived on bread and dripping. Harry, the elder son, later worked at Brasenose College and played in the City of Oxford Orchestra. The younger son is George. At the start of metrication the shop closed. It then stood empty for many years before it was demolished and replaced by Villiers Court flats (see Section 2). This photograph was taken by Mr Charlie Pulker (see Section 13).

George William Cracknell in front of the shop, 56 (originally number 26) Rose Hill. The dog was called Dinah. In the late 1940s, the name was changed to F.P. and G.M. Fagan when Gladys Cracknell (Mrs Fagan) and her husband ran the shop.

Fagan's shop at No. 56 (formerly 26) Rose Hill taken in 1970. It was demolished soon afterwards and replaced by Villiers Court. It was formerly a blacksmith's forge. Many horseshoes were found stored in a shed next to the house. On the right are Nos. 52 and 54 Rose Hill (see Section 2).

Shops at Rose Hill in December 1960. Note the large prams parked outside. (Copyright *Oxford Mail and Times*).

Donna Mazey with her son Connor in July 1999 in front of the Rose Hill shops. Note the modern-style push-chair compared with the prams above.

Part of the Rose Hill shopping frontage in the summer of 1999. Unfortunately, several shops had closed down. In the summer of 1999, a petition signed by 800 people was presented to the Lord Mayor and City Council asking for something to be done about the empty premises.

Rose Hill Post Office, facing the main road, with Michaela, the Postmistress, outside. Taken in 1999.

The Co-operative Society Butcher's shop at Rose Hill in about 1961. On the left is Carol Davis with her son Kevin and on the right Hilary Griffiths with her daughter Mandy.

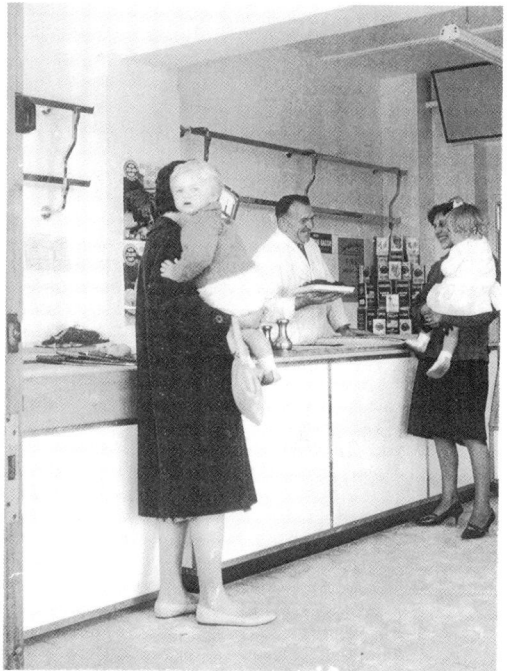

The Co-op shop at the Oval, Rose Hill, in 1961/62. Customers are, left to right: Doreen Shepherd, Mrs Muriel Brown and Mrs Boddington. Serving behind the counter, in the days before self-service and check-outs, are –, Mrs B. Wyatt, Mrs Edna Springer. (The above two photographs courtesy of Mrs Babs Brown.)

The Co-op shop in March 1999. Left to right: Doris Goodwin, Honorary Life Member of the Rose Hill Community Centre, Wendy Gordon, Assistant, who has been at the shop for 25 years, Marc Dawson, Manager, Iris Litten, Vene Mold. David Walton is standing behind.

Mr Earl in the Newsagents at the Oval which, by 1999 when this photograph was taken, he had owned for 13 years.

SECTION THIRTEEN

People

The Pulkers

One of the oldest families in this area, the history of the Pulkers can be traced back to the Middle Ages and beyond. They were a substantial family in Iffley 500 years ago, as is recorded at the time of the death of Walter in 1497. It is thought that the Pulkers came over with William the Conqueror.

William Thomas Pulker (died 1943 at the age of 79) and his wife Alice (died 1945) taken on the occasion of their Golden Wedding in about 1942. They are standing outside No. 8 Rose Hill Cottages which later became 8 Villiers Lane. They were the parents of Bill, Charlie, Bessie, Rose, Lily and May.

Lily Pulker (left) and her sister Bessie in about 1900, taken outside the wash-house of No. 8 Rose Hill Cottages (now Villiers Lane).

Above: the same sisters as in the previous photograph taken about eight years later outside the same wash-house at No. 8 Rose Hill Cottages. Lily Pulker (left) and Bessie (right) with a friend. Note the water-pump and water butt on the right.

A group of Rose Hill residents taken in the early years of the 20th century. Standing on the far right is Charlie Pulker with his brother Bill next to him, seated on the step. In the front on the left is Rose Pulker next to one of her sisters.

Bill Pulker (1892–1972) in the uniform of the Seaforth Highlanders in the First World War. He had earlier served in the Royal Engineers and later in the Tank Regiment. In the Second World War he served in the Home Guard from the start, with the Cowley detachment.

Above: Charlie and Bill Pulker with (on the right) George Henwood, member of an old Iffley family. The photograph was taken in 1918. As Charlie was unfit for military service, he drove ammunition lorries down to the docks. Afterwards he worked for John Allens in Cowley and then in the engine room on Salters steamers. Bill was a master printer at Oxonian Press and was always proud of his Pulker ancestry.

Pulker girls May (left) and Rose also joined up in the First World War. They are both wearing the uniform of the Women's Auxiliary Corps and were both cooks. This was taken in about 1918.

Army Form W. 3677.

N.B.—Any person finding this Certificate is requested to forward it to the Officer i/c Records, W.A.A.C., c/o the Secretary, War Office, S.W.1.

WARNING.—*If you lose this Certificate a duplicate cannot be issued.*

1.   Women's Army Auxiliary Corps.

Character on discharge of No. *23647.*

Name *Pulker Rose Alice.*

Grading *Cook.*

Enrolled at *London.*   on *23-1-18.*

Discharged *Chatham.*   on *28-1-20.*

2.   Work.

Her work during the time she has been in the Corps has been

Excellent

Signature *Campbell*

Date *14-1-20*

3.   Personal Character.

Her personal character during the time she has been in the Corps has been *most satisfactory*

Signature *Campbell*

Date *14-1-20*   [P.T.O.

(7 29 59)   W3013—PP2390   10,000   9/19   HWV(P)
GD2600   10,000   10/19

Rose's discharge papers from the Army in January, 1920 after two years service. Her work was described as 'excellent' and her personal character as 'most satisfactory'.

Charlie Pulker driving a City of Oxford steam-roller in the 1920s. (All Pulker photographs courtesy of Mr Jim Wiblin.)

The Wiblins

The wedding of Rose Pulker and Frederick Wiblin in 1926. They were married at Iffley Church.

Above: Jim Wiblin lived with his parents, Rose (née Pulker) and Frederick, at No. 10 Villiers Lane from 1928 to 1948. He is in the uniform of the Parachute Regiment in which he served in the Second World War. He married Betty Hudson in 1948. Jim was a printer like his uncle Bill amd worked with him at the Oxonian Press.

Jim and Betty Wiblin in 1999. They celebrated their Golden Wedding in August 1998.

The Fagans

Pat Fagan (later Towers) in the garden of No. 52 Rose Hill in April 1932. The house beyond is No. 50 and was once the home of Judge Sale (see page 13).

Mrs Gladys Fagan (née Cracknell) and her daughter Pat in the Summer of 1999. The Cracknell family ran the shop on Rose Hill from 1914 (see Section 12). In the later 1940s, the name of the business was changed to F.P. and G.M. Fagan when Gladys and her husband ran the shop.

Annesley Road residents

The Rowlands

The houses in Annesley Road were built by Pye Ltd. in 1935 and they were originally part of what was known as the Iffley Turn Estate. (See Section 1 for a record of earlier residents in this area in 100 AD).

Elsie and Douglas Rowland were married in Jersey (Elsie's home) on 3rd August 1936. Douglas came from Swindon. In the same year they bought their house in Annesley Road. They had three children, two girls and a boy. When they moved in, the nearest shops were in Between Towns Road in Cowley. A bus came from Oxford to the Westbury Crescent corner. They had friendly neighbours of mixed age groups. The houses had open fires but gas fires in the bedrooms. Elsie is now one of the few remaining original residents of Annesley Road.

Mrs Elsie Rowland in 1999.

The Cartwrights

The Cartwrights were also among the first residents in Annesley Road.

Four girls on the wall of No. 52 Annesley Road, taken in about 1944. Left to right: Frances Cartwright, Delsie ?, Catherine Boyle, Peggy Punnett.

Here, in about 1949, Frances Cartwright (centre back) is seen with her husband Lewis (right). The young Frances (in front) is their daughter. She taught general subjects and country dancing at Rose Hill School from 1973 to 1979. On the left is Father (Ricardo Domez) James from Spain who visited Rose Hill regularly to learn English. (Photographs courtesy of Mr Donald Boyle.)

Miss Frances Cartwright with her brother-in-law Mr Donald Boyle photographed in Annesley Road in 1999. Mr Boyle is wearing the uniform of the 29th Division Association and his medals which he won when he served with the U.S. Army.

The Days

Mrs Hilda Day (née Rawlings) is one of the last of the originals in Annesley Road, having come in 1936. Her father served in the Oxford and Bucks regiment in India and Hilda spent much of her childhood there. Her grandfather, who had also been in the same regiment, was Marshal of Oxford University.

The identical twin sons of Mr and Mrs Day. David (left) and Michael, on the occasion of David's Wedding in November 1968.

Annesley Road parties

Annesley Road Party to celebrate the end of the Second World War in 1945. When the residents heard that the war was almost over they had decided to have a Street Party and when peace was declared on VJ Day plans went ahead. Trestle tables were lent by Cowley barracks and white paper served as table cloths. They had a piano and they also had a big bonfire in the road and were surprised to find a large hole in the surface next morning. Flags were hung right across the road which was floodlit. The photograph, courtesy of Mrs H. Day, was taken by Mr Ronald Day.

After the success of the Party, some residents asked why they could not start a Residents' Association for all the roads on the Iffley Turn Estate. This got going in about 1947 with Mr Ronald Day as its first Chairman, and lasted about 25 years. They had Saturday socials, a Monday dancing class, Thursday whist drives, children's Christmas parties, a drama group for all ages, quizzes and debates. There were day-outings and a fortnight's holiday organised by Mr Day. There was also a Youth Club with its own committee run by teenagers. The events were held in the Iffley Institute until that building was pulled down.

A Residents' Association Christmas Party in about 1946. In the back row, standing, left to right, are: Mrs Harris, –, Mrs Cox, Mrs Murphy, Mrs Day, Mrs Hall, Mr Hart, –, –, –. The men who are dressed up as clowns worked at Morris Motors.

Another Rose Hill Residents' Association Christmas Party in about 1947. (Courtesy Mrs E. Rowland.) Left to right, fifth row: –, –, Barney, –, –, Roy Gibbons, Tony Newbold, –, Mrs Taylor. Others unknown until end of row (right to left): Mrs Gibbons and Colin (next to curtain) Mrs Boyler, –, Mrs Higgins, Pamela Tull. Fourth row: Jean Barney, M(?) Underhill, Valerie Higgins, Ann North, A(?) Underhill, Colin Jarman, two Pulkers(?), Ivor Wheatley, –. –, Joy Henwood. Third row: Alan Hills, Peter Bowles, Marion Thomas, Shirley Burchall, –, Elizabeth Higgins, Barbara Newbold, Jill Birchall, Ann Taylor and brother(?), –, Ann Mawer, Raymond Gould. Second row:–, Jill Harris. –, Jean Howse, –, Joyce Rowland, Wendy Lytton, Susan Mawer, –, –, David Gammon, –, – First row: – and –, –, –, Michael Day, Geoffrey Eaton, David Day, –, Peter Gammon, Timothy Towner, rest not identified.

A Rose Hill Residents Association Outing in about 1949. Left to right: back row: –, Mrs Murphy, –, –. Front row: –, Mrs Veary, Mrs Bowles, Mrs Murphy (sister-in-law of above), –, Mrs Teagle, –, Mrs Norris, Mrs Absalom, Mrs Newbold, Mrs Elsie Rowland. In front: Margaret Rowland. (Above photographs courtesy of Mrs E. Rowland).

The Buckinghams

Mr Bill Buckingham, J.P. (left) talking to Councillor William Gowers, Mayor of Oxford, who was visiting Rose Hill Community Centre for a Fête in 1954/5. Councillor Gowers represented the University in the days when it had councillors on Oxford City Council. This photograph was taken in the old army hut at the Centre which was burnt down not long afterwards. Bill Buckingham, who has given more of his time and talents to Rose Hill than most, became a Councillor for Littlemore and, after that area was included within the City boundaries in 1992, he joined Oxford City Council. It was not long afterwards that he became Lord Mayor of Oxford and he and his wife, who was Lady Mayoress, had a very successful year as Oxford's first citizens.

Councillor Bill Buckingham, former Lord Mayor and President and Secretary of Rose Hill Community Association. Here at the Centre, in January 1999, he is congratulating Mrs Ethel Wheal on her MBE which was awarded to her in 1998 for voluntary work, especially among older people in Rose Hill.

The Browns

Mr Norman Brown and his wife Babs taken in 1967/8 with their grandchildren. Both Mr and Mrs Brown did much for the community of Rose Hill over a period of many years. Mr Brown not only chaired the Community Association but for a long time was editor of the Community's Newsletter which was called *Rose Hill Roundabout*. A hall at the Community Centre is named after him. Grandchildren left to right: Sharon Davis, Kevin Davis, Paul Brown, Russell Brown.

The Bromleys

Alderman Percy Bromley and his wife Betty on the occasion of their Golden Wedding outside their house at No. 65 Courtland Road, Rose Hill. The photograph, courtesy of Mr Ron Bromley, was taken on 8th December 1978. The Bromleys came to Oxford from Dover in 1927/8 where Percy was a Freeman of the town. He spent all his working life as a compositor with the *Oxford Mail and Times*. He was Lord Mayor of Oxford in 1969/70.

Singletree residents

Mrs Betty Ledger (left) who was County Councillor for Littlemore, Sandford and Rose Hill from 1952 to 1972. On the right is Mrs Mabel Harris who was the second person to come into Singletree where this photograph was taken. Both are residents of Singletree which has a thriving and self-supporting Residents' Association. There is a weekly sewing afternoon, bingo twice a week and a monthly evening function. Photograph taken in 1999.

Mrs Ledger (right) with Mrs Barbara Prescott who is known as the catering brains of Singletree. She was formerly cook at the Town Hall and has been at Singletree since the beginning. She still cooks a monthly lunch for the residents. The photograph was taken in the coffee room at Singletree in August 1999. (See Section 2 for more about Singletree.)

The Coopers

Freda and George Cooper at the Rose Hill Garden and Social Club Show in September 1999. (See also Section 6.) They have contributed much to the life of Rose Hill. George was Warden of the Centre from about 1965 to 1974 but still plays a major part in its activities.

The Elseys

Mr (Henry) John Elsey (1921–1999) had the dental surgery on Rose Hill (seen on the right in 1999) from 1948/9 until his retirement in 1989. He was much loved and appreciated. Not only did he run the practice but he lectured on dentistry all over the country and abroad, including Canada and Australia. He was also a Methodist lay preacher.

In 1952 he married Margaret Handley and they are seen on the left on their honeymoon.

John and Margaret Elsey with Simon, one of their three sons. They also had one daughter. This was taken in the mid-1970s at their house in Abberbury Road called 'Mallows'. The photographs are courtesy of Mrs M. Elsey.